Grand Canyon National Park
Adult Coloring Book

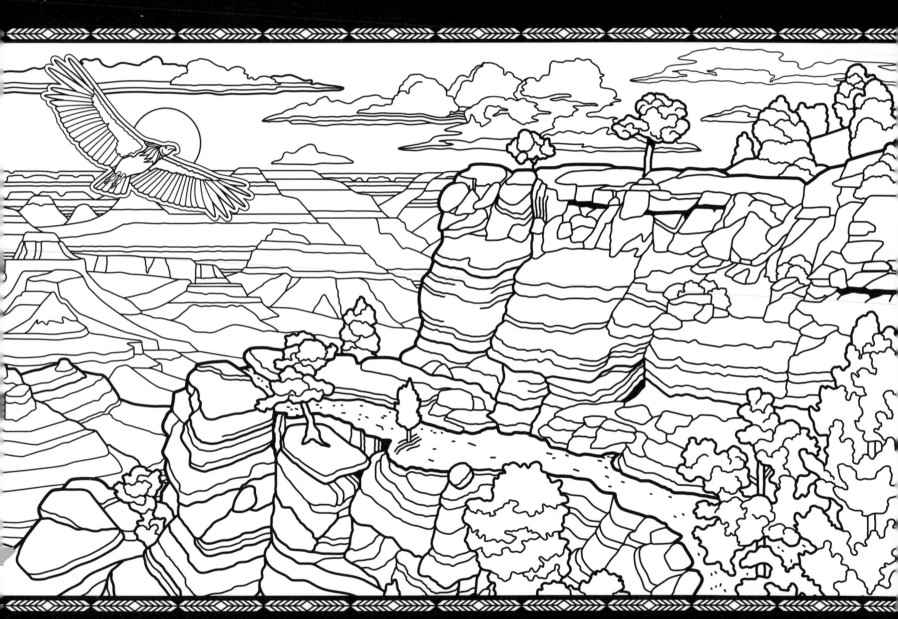

Dave Ember

A Magical Coloring Journey through Grand Canyon National Park

ISBN: 978-1-56037-721-4

For more information about our books, write Farcountry Press, P.O. Box 5630,
Helena, MT 59604; call (800) 821-3874; or visit www.farcountrypress.com.

Produced in the United States of America.
Printed in China.

22 21 20 19 18   1 2 3 4 5 6

The Coloring Artist

of this Book Is:

Grand Canyon National Park

Carved by the Colorado River beginning about six million years ago, the Grand Canyon is a landscape that more than lives up to its name. With its many-hued rock layers that change colors with the light, diverse ecosystems with differing plants and animals, and sound-swallowing air space above a mile-deep chasm, the canyon transcends description. Paleo-Indians first wandered the park 13,000 years ago, hunting, gathering wild foods, and leaving stories painted on or chipped into the rock. Ancestral Puebloans built stone structures and grew crops where they could. Hualapai, Havasupai, Hopi, and other native peoples have made a living here and still live in the canyon or the region.

Soldiers in Coronado's 1540 expedition were the first Europeans to view the canyon. John Wesley Powell famously explored the Colorado River through the canyon in 1869. Miners, ranchers, and adventurers came seeking riches or excitement. In 1901, the Santa Fe Railroad built a rail line to the South Rim for paying tourists, and grand lodges to house them. In 1919, Theodore Roosevelt signed legislation to create Grand Canyon National Park.

Today more than 6 million visitors annually come to witness the canyon's grandeur. The South Rim, with its busy Grand Canyon Village, hosts ninety percent of visitors. The North Rim offers a quieter experience. Visitors can explore the canyon on foot or by mule on hundreds of miles of trails or from below on a river adventure.

Grand Canyon National Park

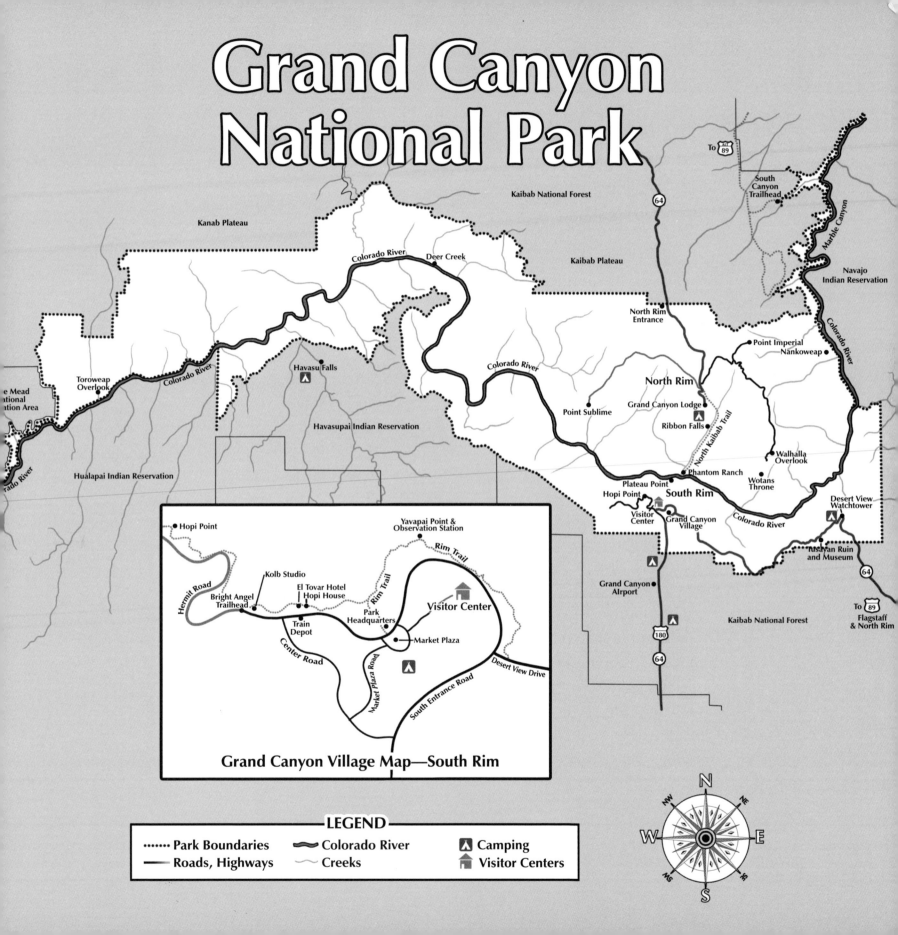

Kaibab National Forest

Kanab Plateau

Colorado River   Deer Creek

Kaibab Plateau

To 89

South Canyon Trailhead

Marble Canyon

North Rim Entrance

Navajo Indian Reservation

Colorado River

Colorado River

Point Imperial
Nankoweap

Colorado River

Toroweap Overlook

Colorado River

North Rim

Grand Canyon Lodge

Point Sublime

Ribbon Falls

North Kaibab Trail

Walhalla Overlook

Havasu Falls

Havasupai Indian Reservation

Mead ational ation Area

Hualapai Indian Reservation

Phantom Ranch

Plateau Point

Hopi Point

South Rim

Wotans Throne

Desert View Watchtower

Visitor Center

Grand Canyon Village

Colorado River

Tusayan Ruin and Museum

Grand Canyon Airport

64

180

Kaibab National Forest

To 89

Flagstaff & North Rim

64

Grand Canyon Village Map—South Rim

Hopi Point

Yavapai Point & Observation Station

Rim Trail

Kolb Studio

El Tovar Hotel
Hopi House

Rim Trail

Hermit Road

Bright Angel Trailhead

Train Depot

Park Headquarters

Visitor Center

Center Road

Market Plaza Road

Market Plaza

Desert View Drive

South Entrance Road

LEGEND

- ······· Park Boundaries
- ──── Roads, Highways
- ∿∿ Colorado River
- ∿ Creeks
- ⛺ Camping
- 🏠 Visitor Centers

N NW NE W E SW SE S

Hiking the North Kaibab Trail from the North Rim can involve a few hours or a multi-day adventure, depending on the destination. The trail descends from the North Rim 13.7 miles to Bright Angel Campground, where hikers can cross the Colorado River and proceed up to the South Rim. Bring plenty of water and don't hike alone. Cliff swallows build gourd-shaped mud nests beneath rock overhangs.

A single beavertail cactus may have hundreds of fleshy, pad-like leaves, with waxy, hot-pink flowers. Instead of spines, it features clusters of small, barbed bristles. The Grand Canyon beavertail is a special status species, so please don't disturb these plants. Among the most common reptiles in the park, spiny lizards can reach twelve inches in length. Watch for them basking in the sun on rocky outcrops.

Habitat loss, shooting, lead poisoning, and other hazards led to the near extinction of the California condor, the largest bird in North America. A much-larger cousin of the turkey vulture, it has black and white wings and a wingspan of up to nine and a half feet. Condors were re-introduced to Arizona in 1996. The first wild nesting since reintroduction was at the park in 2001.

Built at Bright Angel Point with a magnificent canyon viewpoint, Grand Canyon Lodge is the only lodge on the North Rim. Constructed in 1928 of logs and native Kaibab limestone, its cabins and main lodge retain a rustic, western atmosphere from the early days of national park tourism. Both golden-mantled and spotted ground squirrels live in the park. They may be cute, but be sure never to feed them or any park wildlife.

Mountain lions are the largest predators in the park, resting and sheltering from the sun on rock ledges, in small caves, or beneath vegetation. They find water in small pools and rocky catch basins, or at the river. Biologists are studying how mountain lions and desert bighorn sheep, their prey, interact. A lion's long, heavy tail helps it balance as it moves about the canyon's rocky habitat.

Ancestral Puebloans built the Nankoweap Granaries—grain and seed storage rooms—700 feet above the Colorado River in Marble Canyon. The site, constructed of rock between the years 1050 and 1150, is accessible by the long and unmaintained Nankoweap Trail or by boat. Visitors shouldn't enter, touch, or disturb the ruins. Peregrine falcons plummet through canyon airspace after swifts, swallows, and other avian prey.

Rushing whitewater, stunning views of towering rock walls, and glimpses of canyon plants and wildlife make rafting the Colorado River through the Grand Canyon an amazing experience. River trips offered by commercial outfitters range from half day floats of smooth water to nineteen-day river adventures that cover 226 miles. Whether by large motorized raft, oared raft, paddle raft, or dory, each trip is unique.

Most bats emerge after sundown, but the canyon bat (Parastrellus hesperus) is often seen in shadowed canyons in late afternoon or early evening, foraging along canyon walls and over boulders and shrubs in slow, butterfly-like flight. Watch the park's night skies for some of the twenty-two different bat species inhabiting the Grand Canyon. Abandoned mines dating from the canyon's mining era provide excellent roost sites for many bats.

Located on the South Rim near the Bright Angel Lodge, the Kolb Studio was the home and photography studio of Ellsworth and Emery Kolb. The brothers arrived at the Grand Canyon in 1901, pitching a tent on the South Rim and later building a small, wooden house and studio. Between 1904 and 1926, they pioneered photography of the Grand Canyon and Colorado River.

With its stunning views, historic lodges, and bustling Grand Canyon Village, the South Rim hosts ninety percent of park visitors. Located on the "Arizona" side of the canyon, it is easier to get to than the North Rim, open year round, and has abundant visitor services and activities. The South Rim is also more crowded so visitors should plan well ahead, especially during the summer season.

Raccoons, sometimes nicknamed "masked bandits," are common at campgrounds on both canyon rims, where they can become pests by raiding campsites and picnic tables. These mostly nocturnal omnivores favor habitats near water. Excellent climbers, raccoons are equally adept at scaling trees and rocky cliffs.

Geologists located the historic Yavapai Observation Station at an outstanding place along the South Rim to observe and understand Grand Canyon geology. Because of its wide variety of ecosystems, Grand Canyon National Park is home to an incredible diversity of bird life with nearly 450 species of birds. Pictured left to right are: western tanager, Clark's nutcracker, western meadowlark, ash-throated flycatcher, and black-throated gray warbler.

The El Tovar Hotel, which opened on the South Rim in 1905, is considered the crown jewel of national park lodges. Architect Charles Whittlesey designed it as a mixture of Swiss chalet and Norwegian villa to appeal to travelers of the time, who preferred European luxury to rustic western charm. Rocky Mountain elk were introduced into Arizona in the early 1900s, and some eventually entered the park. They may appear docile but can be dangerous, so view them from at least 100 feet.

You aren't likely to see a ringtail, Arizona's state mammal, though they are common park residents. These cat-sized predators rest during the day, emerging to hunt wood-rats and other prey during the cooler night. Their black-and-white-ringed bushy tails are as long as their head and body combined. Nimble climbers, ringtails leap, ricochet, and chimney-climb around rugged canyons and cliffs.

The Grand Canyon Railway first began
bringing tourists to the canyon in 1901.
Its owner, the Santa Fe Railroad, also built
grand hotels on the South Rim to house
guests brought there by train. Visitors can
relive park history by travelling the sixty-five
miles between Williams and the South Rim
on restored rail cars, an eight-hour ride
round-trip.

Descending into the canyon on a mule ride is a classic way to see the Grand Canyon. Rides leave from both rims and vary from a half-day trip to overnight rides that go deep into the canyon. There are age and size restrictions, and advance reservations are recommended. The Bright Angel Trail descends 9.5 miles and 4,340 feet from the South Rim to Bright Angel Campground.

The humpback chub, a native fish of the Colorado River, became endangered after damming changed the river's ecology. Native fish are adapted to spring flooding, but dams controlled this, making it harder for the fish to spawn. Park biologists have been relocating native fish to downstream tributaries in the western Grand Canyon. Here warmer water and fewer nonnative predators provide better conditions for the fish to spawn.

In the canyon's desert environment, Ribbon Falls offers a spectacular surprise along the North Kaibab Trail. Hidden in a side canyon, the shining ribbon of water cascades 100 feet to splash onto a travertine spire built up from minerals in the water. The falls is 7.9 miles from the North Kaibab Trailhead. Visitors should plan to stay overnight at Cottonwood Campground or farther down the canyon at Phantom Ranch or Bright Angel Campground.

Abert's squirrel is one of the most common mammals in the park, found wherever Ponderosa pines grow. A subspecies, the Kaibab squirrel, shares similar characteristics but is found only on the Kaibab Plateau on the north side of the Grand Canyon. Plateau Point offers a spectacular viewpoint of the inner canyon from the Bright Angel Trail, 6.1 miles and 3,080 feet below the trailhead on the South Rim.

A rainbow of wildflowers paints the park in every color spring through fall, including orange globe mallow and blue Grand Canyon phacelia. Visitors hiking off trail can unknowingly trample rare plants like the endangered sentry milk-vetch, which grows only in narrow bands along the canyon's edge. Wildflower guides are available in park gift shops and checklists can be down-loaded or found at park visitor centers.

Mary Elizabeth Jane Colter, renowned architect of many park buildings, patterned Desert View Watchtower after Ancestral Puebloan towers at Hovenweep and Mesa Verde National Parks. Designed to blend into the landscape, it is built of native stone with a steel internal framework. Visitors can climb the tower for panoramic views of more than 100 miles on a clear day, including the Painted Desert to the east.

The Point Imperial Trail reaches 8,803 feet, the highest point on the North Rim, with views of the Painted Desert, Marble Canyon, and eastern Grand Canyon. Ancient Precambrian rock layers paint the canyon red and black, while red, black, and yellow western tanagers bring color, energy, and song to the landscape. Cottontails are common throughout the park, providing food for coyotes, hawks, and other predators.

A world famous resort built at the bottom of the Grand Canyon, Phantom Ranch offers guests the experience of an earlier time in the West. Guests must travel by foot, mule, or boat for a stay in the ranch's stone cabins or dormitory. Reservations must be made by online lottery, beginning fifteen months in advance. Mule deer are named for their long, mule-like ears.

The stunning Wotans Throne is an isolated sandstone formation on the North Rim, rising to 7,633 feet. Cape Royal offers a prime viewpoint, though the formation is also visible from the South Rim. Wotan is the name, in Old High German, for the Norse god Odin. The throne is a popular subject of landscape photographers for its stunning color and texture, especially at sunrise and sunset.

The 292 species of butterflies and moths in the park are important pollinators of flowering plants. Most often seen from early June to mid-August, they are found throughout the park, from the Colorado River up to the tops of both rims. The rare black Kaibab swallowtail is endemic to the North Rim. The brown Mead's wood-nymph is found in piñon-juniper and open pine forests.

The tip of Hopi Point offers a spectacular spot to enjoy a Grand Canyon sunset, with the canyon depths all around. Visitors can walk the trail west from Bright Angel Lodge or ride the free park shuttle. Common throughout the park, ravens are particularly visible at the rims, where they soar in canyon airspace. Agile fliers, ravens can even fly upside down.

Crystalline water streaming from Deer Spring flows down Deer Creek through stunning side canyons. Gushing out of red sandstone, it plunges 180 feet, forming the spectacular Deer Creek Falls. This remote, backcountry site isn't easy to get to but draws backpackers and many day hikers from river trips. Camping is allowed only in designated sites and a back-country permit is required for an overnight stay.

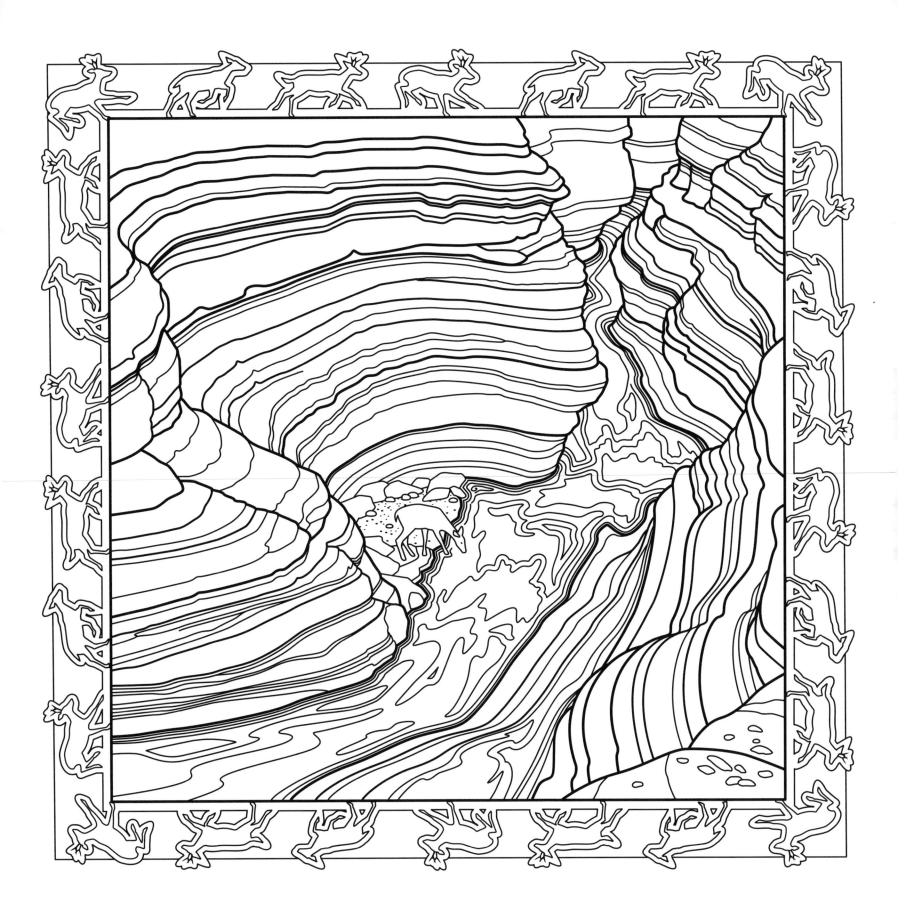

Iconic Grand Canyon architect Mary Colter designed Hopi House, the park's largest gift store, after an ancient pueblo-style Hopi dwelling. Opened in 1905, it is built of stone, with multiple stepped-back roofs, sapling and mud ceilings set on peeled log beams, corner fireplaces, and walls finished in mud plaster. The store offers authentic Native American handicrafts, with a Native American art gallery upstairs.

Inhabiting a landscape of limited resources, desert bighorn sheep are smaller and paler than Rocky Mountain bighorn sheep, with more slender horns. They can go long periods without drinking water. Nimble footed, these sheep favor steep terrain and cliffs, the better to avoid predators such as mountain lions.

Visiting Grand Canyon National Park

Plan ahead by checking the National Park Service website, www.nps.gov/grca, and click on Plan Your Visit for directions to the park, places to go, where to stay, things to do, how to be safe during your visit, and downloadable publications Trip Planner, South Rim Pocket Map, North Rim Pocket Map, and others. The South Rim is open year-round. The North Rim is open seasonally from May 15 to October 31. Reserve rooms in one of the park lodges well in advance of your trip. Advance reservations for Phantom Ranch are required and can be made through Xanterra via online lottery fifteen months in advance. You can reserve a campsite at three of the park's four developed campgrounds, or at a back-country site. Desert View Campground is first come, first served only. Trailer Village is the only campground with full RV hook-ups.

Use the free park shuttle to access overlooks along the South Rim, or walk the 2.1-mile, paved Canyon Rim Trail between Mather Point and South Kaibab Trailhead. Hermit Rest Road heads west of Grand Canyon Village for 7 miles. Desert View Drive heads east of the village 25 miles to the park's east entrance. The hike through the canyon from rim to rim is 21 miles. By car, the shortest route is a five-hour, 220-mile drive. You can also visit tribal lands outside the park that offer visitor services, including the Skywalk.

Get further involved with the park through the Grand Canyon Association, a nonprofit that supports preservation, education, and research. For more information, go to www.grandcanyon.org.

Bring this coloring book with you and check your artistry against nature's spectacular creation, Grand Canyon National Park.

For better support, leave the postcards and bookmarks intact
until you have completed the last few coloring images.

Grand Canyon National Park Facts

Established as a national monument in 1908, designated a national park in 1919.

The Grand Canyon is a World Heritage Site and an International Dark Sky Park.

The park encompasses 1,217,403 acres (1,904 square miles). It averages one mile in depth and ten miles in width rim to rim.

The South Rim lies at 7,000 feet, the North Rim at 8,000 feet. The Colorado River meanders 277 miles through the park at the canyon bottom.

The park is home to nearly 450 species of birds, 92 species of mammals, 18 species of fish (5 native), and 57 species of reptiles and amphibians.

The park hosted 6.25 million visitors in 2017, the second most visited park in the country.

Hikers can explore 358 miles of trails, of which 126 mile are maintained.

Grand Canyon National Park
Adult Coloring Book

Grand Canyon National Park Adult Coloring Book
Postcard Colored by _____

POSTCARD

PLACE STAMP HERE

Address

Grand Canyon National Park Adult Coloring Book
Postcard Colored by _____

POSTCARD

PLACE STAMP HERE

Address

For better support, leave the postcards and bookmarks intact
until you have completed the last few coloring images.

Grand Canyon National Park Facts

Established as a national monument in 1908, designated a national park in 1919.

The Grand Canyon is a World Heritage Site and an International Dark Sky Park.

The park encompasses 1,217,403 acres (1,904 square miles). It averages one mile in depth and ten miles in width rim to rim.

The South Rim lies at 7,000 feet, the North Rim at 8,000 feet. The Colorado River meanders 277 miles through the park at the canyon bottom.

The park is home to nearly 450 species of birds, 92 species of mammals, 18 species of fish (5 native), and 57 species of reptiles and amphibians.

The park hosted 6.25 million visitors in 2017, the second most visited park in the country.

Hikers can explore 358 miles of trails, of which 126 mile are maintained.

Grand Canyon National Park Adult Coloring Book

Grand Canyon National Park Adult Coloring Book
Postcard Colored by _____

POSTCARD

PLACE STAMP HERE

Address

Grand Canyon National Park Adult Coloring Book
Postcard Colored by _____

POSTCARD

PLACE STAMP HERE

Address

For better support, leave the postcards and bookmarks intact
until you have completed the last few coloring images.

Grand Canyon National Park Facts

Established as a national monument in 1908, designated a national park in 1919.

The Grand Canyon is a World Heritage Site and an International Dark Sky Park.

The park encompasses 1,217,403 acres (1,904 square miles). It averages one mile in depth and ten miles in width rim to rim.

The South Rim lies at 7,000 feet, the North Rim at 8,000 feet. The Colorado River meanders 277 miles through the park at the canyon bottom.

The park is home to nearly 450 species of birds, 92 species of mammals, 18 species of fish (5 native), and 57 species of reptiles and amphibians.

The park hosted 6.25 million visitors in 2017, the second most visited park in the country.

Hikers can explore 358 miles of trails, of which 126 mile are maintained.

Grand Canyon National Park Adult Coloring Book

POSTCARD

Grand Canyon National Park Adult Coloring Book
Postcard Colored by

PLACE STAMP HERE

Address

POSTCARD

Grand Canyon National Park Adult Coloring Book
Postcard Colored by

PLACE STAMP HERE

Address

For better support, leave the postcards and bookmarks intact
until you have completed the last few coloring images.

Grand Canyon National Park Facts

Established as a national monument in 1908, designated a national park in 1919.

The Grand Canyon is a World Heritage Site and an International Dark Sky Park.

The park encompasses 1,217,403 acres (1,904 square miles). It averages one mile in depth and ten miles in width rim to rim.

The South Rim lies at 7,000 feet, the North Rim at 8,000 feet. The Colorado River meanders 277 miles through the park at the canyon bottom.

The park is home to nearly 450 species of birds, 92 species of mammals, 18 species of fish (5 native), and 57 species of reptiles and amphibians.

The park hosted 6.25 million visitors in 2017, the second most visited park in the country.

Hikers can explore 358 miles of trails, of which 126 mile are maintained.

Grand Canyon National Park Adult Coloring Book

POSTCARD

Grand Canyon National Park Adult Coloring Book
Postcard Colored by _____

PLACE STAMP HERE

Address

POSTCARD

Grand Canyon National Park Adult Coloring Book
Postcard Colored by _____

PLACE STAMP HERE

Address